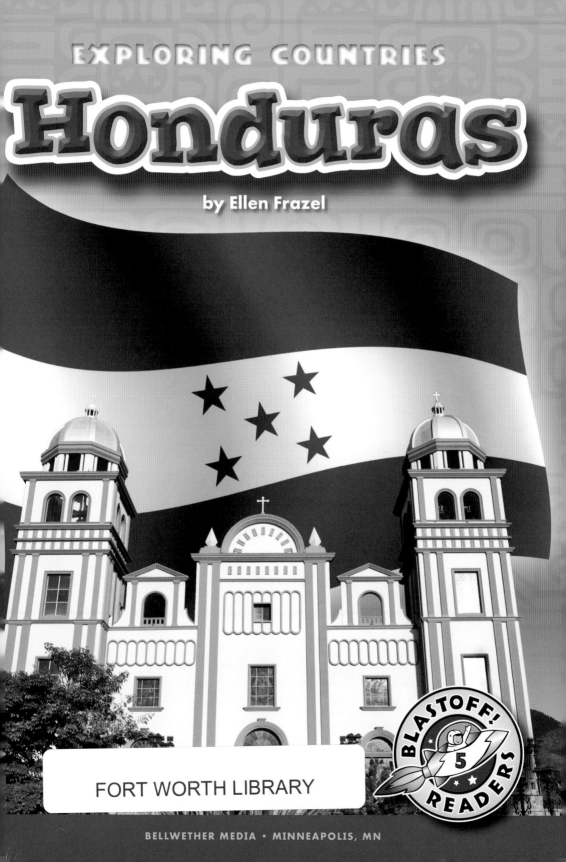

EXPLORING COUNTRIES

Honduras

by Ellen Frazel

FORT WORTH LIBRARY

BELLWETHER MEDIA • MINNEAPOLIS, MN

Note to Librarians, Teachers, and Parents:

Blastoff! Readers are carefully developed by literacy experts and combine standards based content with developmentally appropriate text.

Level 1 provides the most support through repetition of high-frequency words, light text, predictable sentence patterns, and strong visual support.

Level 2 offers early readers a bit more challenge through varied simple sentences, increased text load, and less repetition of high-frequency words.

Level 3 advances early-fluent readers toward fluency through increased text and concept load, less reliance on visuals, longer sentences, and more literary language.

Level 4 builds reading stamina by providing more text per page, increased use of punctuation, greater variation in sentence patterns, and increasingly challenging vocabulary.

Level 5 encourages children to move from "learning to read" to "reading to learn" by providing even more text, varied writing styles, and less familiar topics.

Whichever book is right for your reader, Blastoff! Readers are the perfect books to build confidence and encourage a love of reading that will last a lifetime!

This edition first published in 2013 by Bellwether Media, Inc.

No part of this publication may be reproduced in whole or in part without written permission of the publisher. For information regarding permission, write to Bellwether Media, Inc., Attention: Permissions Department, 5357 Penn Avenue South, Minneapolis, MN 55419.

Library of Congress Cataloging-in-Publication Data

Frazel, Ellen.
 Honduras / by Ellen Frazel.
   p. cm. – (Blastoff! readers: Exploring countries)
 Includes bibliographical references and index.
 Summary: "Developed by literacy experts for students in grades three through seven, this book introduces young readers to the geography and culture of Honduras"–Provided by publisher.
 ISBN 978-1-60014-860-6 (hardcover : alk. paper)
 1. Honduras–Juvenile literature. I. Title. II. Series: Blastoff! readers. 5, Exploring countries.
 F1503.2.F73 2013
 972.83–dc23   2012029450

Printed in the United States of America, North Mankato, MN.

Contents

Honduras is a country that spans 43,278 square miles (112,090 square kilometers) in Central America. Its capital is Tegucigalpa. Guatemala and El Salvador are its neighbors to the west. Nicaragua borders Honduras to the southeast.

The Caribbean Sea washes onto the country's northern coast. In the south, the **Gulf** of Fonseca curves into the land. Through this gulf lies the Pacific Ocean.

Guatemala

El Salvador

Pacific Ocean

Caribbean
Sea

Did you know?
The Bay Islands lie off the northern coast of Honduras. They are an extension of the Sierra de Omoa mountain range on the mainland.

Honduras

Tegucigalpa ★

Nicaragua

Gulf
of
onseca

N
W — E
S

Did you know?
The tallest peak in Honduras is near the border of El Salvador in the Sierra de Celaque. Cerro Las Minas rises 9,416 feet (2,870 meters) into the sky.

Honduras is a mountainous country. Many mountain ranges rise throughout the center of the land. River valleys cut into the mountains, which generally run from east to west. These valleys contain grassy woodlands where people raise livestock and grow crops.

Coco River

The central highlands slope into narrow lowland stretches along the Pacific coast. In the north, they give way to coastal **plains**. A lowland jungle called La Mosquitia covers the northeastern corner of Honduras. The Coco River flows along the border with Nicaragua there.

fun fact

The Miskito people live in La Mosquitia. Many Miskito make their living diving for lobsters off the coast.

La Mosquitia is part of the Mosquito Coast, a narrow stretch of land that runs from eastern Nicaragua into northeastern Honduras. La Mosquitia contains the largest untouched wilderness area in Central America. **Tropical rain forests** flourish because of the hot and humid weather. **Savannahs** and **mangrove forests** can also be found there.

The Río Plátano Biosphere Reserve is 2,027 square miles (5,250 square kilometers) of protected land in La Mosquitia. The Plátano River runs along this land. The reserve is home to jaguars, giant anteaters, and other rare animals. The **endangered** Central American tapir also roams these forests.

Did you know?
Visitors can take rafting trips down the Plátano River to see the beautiful sights of the Río Plátano Biosphere Reserve.

West Indian manatee

quetzal

three-toed sloth

A variety of animals live in different **habitats** throughout Honduras. Three-toed sloths and spider monkeys hang from tree branches in **cloud forests**. Quetzals and emerald toucanets fly overhead.

kinkajou

Scarlet macaws, king vultures, and harpy eagles soar over the rain forests of La Mosquitia. Ocelots and margays are small spotted cats that roam the forest floor. Off the coast, the endangered West Indian manatee swims in the Caribbean Sea. Whale sharks, bottlenose dolphins, and parrot fish can be found among **coral reefs** near the Bay Islands.

Did you know?

The Garífuna people are descendants of African slaves and Amerindians. They live along the Caribbean coast and are known for their distinct food, music, and dance.

Over 8 million people live in Honduras. Nine out of every ten are *mestizo*, a mix of European and **Amerindian**. A small part of the population is completely Amerindian. There are several official groups of **native** peoples. The Lenca, who live in the southwestern part of the country, make up the largest group. These groups have their own languages and cultures. However, the Spanish language is shared by people throughout Honduras.

Speak Spanish!

English	Spanish	How to say it
hello	hola	OH-lah
good-bye	adiós	ah-dee-OHS
yes	sí	SEE
no	no	NOH
please	por favor	POHR fah-VOR
thank you	gracias	GRAH-see-uhs
friend (male)	amigo	ah-MEE-goh
friend (female)	amiga	ah-MEE-gah

Many Hondurans make their homes in the highlands. They live in brick houses and apartment buildings. Most cities have a central **plaza** where people meet and businesses set up shops. People walk, drive cars, or take buses to get from place to place.

In the countryside, families live in **adobe** houses with straw roofs. Many have breezy porches with hammocks strung up for relaxing after a day of hard work. Small villages also have a central gathering place. It is usually near a soccer field or a few stores. People like to meet here in the afternoons to talk and unwind.

Where People Live in Honduras

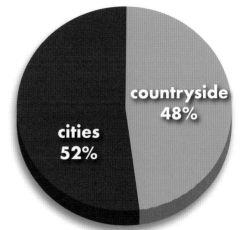

countryside
48%

cities
52%

! fun fact

People in the countryside often build their kitchen outside of the house. It is a room with a wood fire built on the floor or on a platform.

Children in Honduras are required to go to school for six years. However, many families in the countryside need their children to help with farm work and household chores. Students who are able to attend school learn to read, write, and do math problems.

After primary school, students go on to five or six years of secondary school. The first three years focus on advanced math, science, and reading. Students can then choose to learn about accounting, business, or other specific careers. Others work to receive a high school diploma so they can go on to a university.

fun fact

The National Autonomous University of Honduras is the largest university in the country. It has schools in several major cities, including the capital.

17

Where People Work in Honduras

farming 39%

manufacturing 21%

services 40%

Nearly 4 in every 10 Hondurans work as farmers. They grow bananas, pineapples, and other fruits. Many families make their living growing coffee beans. Other farmers plant corn and sugarcane. Off the coasts, people fish for shrimp, tilapia, and lobster.

In cities, some Hondurans work in factories making **textiles**. Others work with lumber to manufacture wood products. Many people have **service jobs**. They own shops where people buy groceries and other goods. Some work in banks and restaurants. Others run hotels that attract **tourists** who want to experience the sights of Honduras.

fun fact

The Honduran national soccer team qualified for the World Cup in 2010.

Hondurans love soccer, or *fútbol*. People often gather in the center of town in the afternoons to have a soft drink and watch children play ball. Hondurans can also join local clubs or leagues. Tennis, baseball, and volleyball are other popular sports.

In cities, people like to relax and hang out with friends and family. They listen to upbeat music like salsa, merengue, and **reggaeton**. Hondurans also like to make crafts. Colorful jewelry and bright clay animals can be found in markets throughout the country.

A meal in Honduras is not complete without beans and tortillas. For breakfast, many people eat the *plato típico*, or typical plate. This includes refried beans, eggs, cheese, fried plantains, and a piece of sausage or bacon. Tortillas and a sweet, thick cream called *mantequilla* are served alongside.

A lunch plate usually features beef or chicken served with rice, beans, and tortillas. Meat at dinnertime may be covered in grilled onions or tomato sauce. On the northern coast, *ceviche de pescado* is popular. This is fish soaked in garlic, lime juice, and seasonings. *Tres leches* cake is made with sweetened milk and enjoyed by people across the country.

fun fact

Garífuna people on the northern coast are known for their *pan de coco*. This dense, sweet bread is made with fresh coconut. Women and children often sell it on the street.

ceviche de pescado

pan de coco

Most Hondurans are **Catholic**. They celebrate Christmas, Easter, and other religious holidays. For Easter, celebrations last for two weeks and include parades and festivals. People travel to the beach with friends and family. Many cities also have holidays honoring their **patron saints**. On the northern coast they celebrate Saint Isidore, the patron saint of farmers, for a week in May. Little carnivals, or *carnavalitos*, take place every night. On Saturday, people come from all over the world to see the floats of the big parade.

On September 15, all Hondurans celebrate Independence Day. Marching bands play on the streets early in the morning. *Fiesta Catracha* also takes place on this day. People gather to share a traditional Honduran meal together.

fun fact

Día del Niño, or Children's Day, is on September 10. Children receive presents and have parties. Some neighborhoods break piñatas filled with treats!

Independence Day

The Copán Ruins stand in western Honduras near the border of Guatemala. They are some of the most **intricate** Mayan ruins in the world. Several large plazas hold temples and altars that give visitors a glimpse of Mayan culture.

stela

One of the most famous sights is the **Hieroglyphic** Stairway. The symbols carved into these steps tell the story of the ancient Mayan city of Copán. The Copán Ruins are one of the first stops for many people traveling in Honduras. They are a great starting point for a journey into the country's exciting history and culture.

Fast Facts About Honduras

Honduras's Flag

The Honduran flag has three horizontal stripes. The top and bottom stripes are blue, and the middle stripe is white. In the middle of the white stripe are five stars arranged in an X. The stars symbolize the countries of the former Federal Republic of Central America. The blue bands represent the Caribbean Sea and the Pacific Ocean. The white band stands for land, peace, and prosperity.

Official Name: Republic of Honduras

Area: 43,278 square miles (112,090 square kilometers); Honduras is the 103rd largest country in the world.

Capital City:	Tegucigalpa
Important Cities:	San Pedro Sula, Choloma, La Ceiba
Population:	8,296,693 (July 2012)
Official Language:	Spanish
National Holiday:	Independence Day (September 15)
Religions:	Roman Catholic (97%), Protestant (3%)
Major Industries:	farming, mining, fishing, services
Natural Resources:	lumber, coal, hydropower, gold, silver, copper, iron, zinc
Manufactured Products:	wood products, clothing products, food products
Farm Products:	bananas, coffee beans, citrus, corn, beef, shrimp, tilapia, lobster
Unit of Money:	lempira; the lempira is divided into 100 centavos.

Glossary

adobe—bricks made of clay and straw that are dried in the sun

Amerindian—descending from native people who have lived in North and South America since before Europeans settled

Catholic—belonging to the Roman Catholic Church; Roman Catholics are Christian.

cloud forests—tropical mountain forests that are covered by clouds and fog

coral reefs—structures made of coral that usually grow in shallow seawater

endangered—at risk of becoming extinct

gulf—a part of an ocean or sea that extends into land

habitats—the environments in which plants or animals usually live

hieroglyphic—written in hieroglyphs; hieroglyphs are little pictures, or characters, used in ancient writing.

intricate—very detailed

mangrove forests—swampy areas of trees and shrubs along coastline

native—originally from a certain place

patron saints—saints who are believed to look after a country or group of people

plains—large areas of flat land

plaza—an open space in the middle of a city or town where people gather

reggaeton—a form of music that comes from Latin and Caribbean styles; reggaeton blends hip hop, salsa, reggae, and other music.

savannahs—grasslands with scattered trees

service jobs—jobs that perform tasks for people or businesses

textiles—fabrics or clothes that have been woven or knitted

tourists—people who travel to visit another country

tropical rain forests—thick, green forests in the hot and wet regions near the equator

To Learn More

AT THE LIBRARY
McGaffey, Leta. *Honduras.* New York, N.Y.:
Marshall Cavendish Benchmark, 2010.

Shields, Charles J. *Honduras.* Broomall, Pa.: Mason
Crest Publishers, 2009.

Zuchora-Walske, Christine. *Honduras in Pictures.*
Minneapolis, Minn.: Twenty-First Century Books,
2010.

ON THE WEB
Learning more about Honduras
is as easy as 1, 2, 3.

1. Go to www.factsurfer.com.

2. Enter "Honduras" into the search box.

3. Click the "Surf" button and you will see a list of
   related Web sites.

With factsurfer.com, finding more information is just
a click away.

Index